MY PET

Kitten

Honor Head

Photographs by Jane Burton

636.8

Belitha Press

1172426 9

First published in the UK in 2000 by
Belitha Press
An imprint of Chrysalis Books plc
64 Brewery Road, London N7 9NT

Paperback edition first published in 2002

ISBN 1 84138 083 0 (hardback)
ISBN 1 84138 355 4 (paperback)

British Library Cataloguing in
Publication Data for this book
is available from the British Library.

Editor: Claire Edwards
Designer: Rosamund Saunders
Illustrator: Pauline Bayne
Consultant: Frazer Swift

Printed in Hong Kong

10 9 8 7 6 5 4 3 (hb)
10 9 8 7 6 5 4 3 2 (pb)

PDSA (People's Dispensary for Sick Animals)
is Britain's largest charity which each year
provides free treatment for some 1.4 million
sick and injured animals of disadvantaged
owners.

A royalty of 2.5 per cent of the proceeds from
this book will be paid to the PDSA (People's
Dispensary for Sick Animals) on every copy
sold in the UK.

The products featured have been kindly
donated by Pets at Home.

Contents

Owning your own pet   5

Different types of cat   6

A pregnant cat   8

Newborn kittens   10

Kittens grow quickly   12

Kittens like to play   14

Looking after your kitten   16

How to handle your kitten   18

Kittens like to keep clean   20

Kittens enjoy exploring   22

Visiting the vet   24

How is your kitten feeling?   26

Kittens become cats   28

Words to remember   30

Index   31

Notes for parents   32

My kitten

whiskers

collar and
name tag

fur

tail

paws

It's fun owning your own pet.

Kittens look very sweet and are fun to play with, but they need to be looked after carefully.

A kitten needs feeding every day and brushing regularly. It will also have to be trained. Most of all, remember that your kitten will grow into a cat and be with you for a long time.

Young children with pets should always be supervised by an adult. For further notes, please see page 32.

There are many different types of cats.

Long-haired cats look pretty and fluffy, but they need to be combed and brushed every day. This is called grooming.

Short-haired cats do not need to be groomed so often.

Cats have many different colours and markings.

This is a tortoiseshell.

This is a ginger cat.

This is a tabby cat.

There are many different kinds of cat. Siamese cats have short, sleek fur and a long, pointed face. Ragdoll cats are bigger and very fluffy.

A pregnant cat needs somewhere safe to have her kittens.

A pregnant cat will look for a quiet and safe place to have her kittens. An old blanket or some torn-up newspaper will make her feel more comfortable.

When a cat becomes pregnant her shape changes. Her stomach grows bigger and rounder.

When she is very pregnant, a mother cat doesn't move about much. She may be stroked gently, but not picked up.

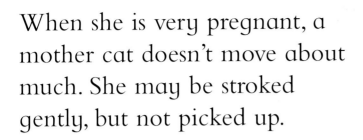

When a mother cat is ready to have her kittens, she stops eating. Soon she will have her first kitten. It will take a long time for all the kittens to be born.

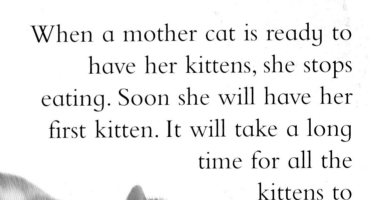

When kittens are born, they can't see, hear or walk.

A newborn kitten
is a terrible mess!
Its mother soon
licks it clean.

Kittens find their way to their mother's milk by smell. Drinking their mother's milk is called suckling. Kittens first start to purr when they are suckling.

When they have finished feeding, the kittens fall asleep in a heap. The mother cat goes off to eat and rest. The kittens look sweet but they are too young to be touched.

If a kitten feels lost or frightened it will miaow loudly for its mother.

Kittens grow very quickly.

The mother cat moves her kittens by picking them up in her mouth. People should never pick up a kitten or a cat by the neck.

When a kitten is one week old it cannot walk properly and crawls along the floor.

The mother cat keeps her kittens clean by licking them. This also teaches the kittens how to lick themselves clean.

At three weeks the kitten is learning to walk. It is very wobbly on its legs and keeps falling over.

When the kitten is eight weeks old, it is old enough to leave its mother.

When the kitten is six weeks old it can run and jump and begin to explore its home.

Kittens are very playful.

As the kittens grow older they begin to play together. They pretend to fight, but they don't hurt each other.

The mother cat teaches her kittens how to hunt and pounce by playing with a toy mouse.

If a kitten is healthy and happy it will always find something to play with.

Kittens will love playing with you as long as you are gentle. Play with a special cat toy or a piece of string or ball of paper.

Make sure your kitten's toys are safe. They should have no metal or sharp bits.

You have to look after your kitten.

Your kitten must be trained to use a litter tray. Put the litter tray in a quiet, private place.

Kittens need small meals four times a day. Always keep the bowls clean and rinse them well after you have washed them.

By eight weeks, kittens can eat solid food. Leave your pet alone when it is eating. Always give your kitten clean, fresh water to drink.

Make sure your pet has a quiet, warm place to sleep. Put a blanket or a squashy cushion in a basket or box.

Be gentle with your kitten.

Do not make your kitten jump. Hold out your hand for it to sniff then pick it up gently. If it doesn't want to be picked up, leave it alone.

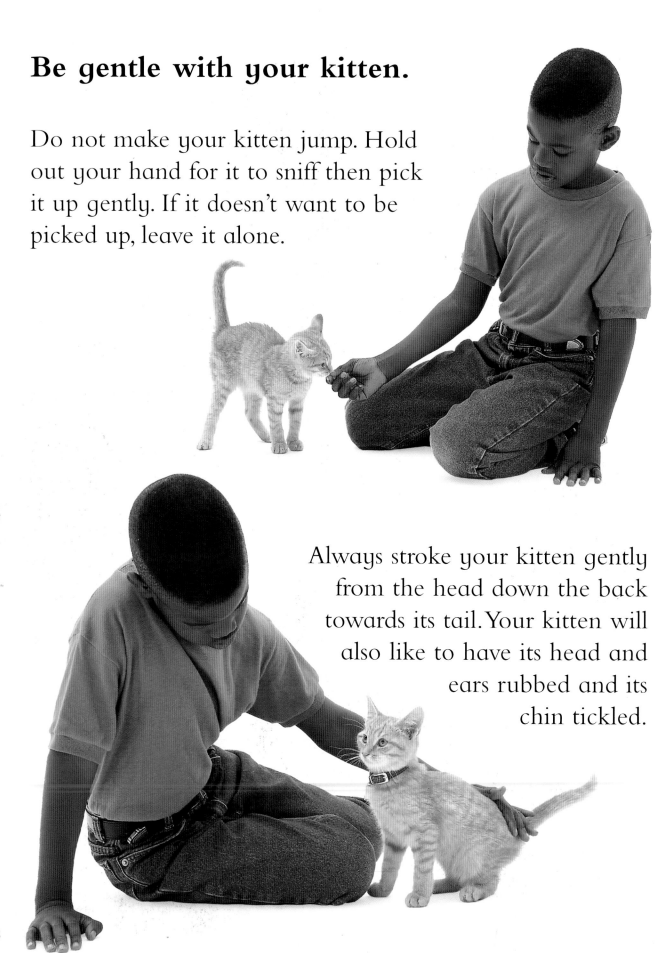

Always stroke your kitten gently from the head down the back towards its tail. Your kitten will also like to have its head and ears rubbed and its chin tickled.

When you pick up your kitten, hold it under its bottom with one hand and gently support its body with the other hand. Do not squeeze it around the middle with its legs dangling.

Never grab your kitten or pull its tail. Your kitten is small and you might hurt it.

Kittens like to keep clean.

A kitten spends a lot of time cleaning itself. It uses its paws to wash its face. It licks its fur to keep it smooth.

Comb and brush your kitten from the head towards the tail. Comb it gently, then brush it. If it has any knots you can't untangle, take it to the vet. Never pull its fur.

Most kittens enjoy being brushed if you are gentle. Use a special brush and comb.

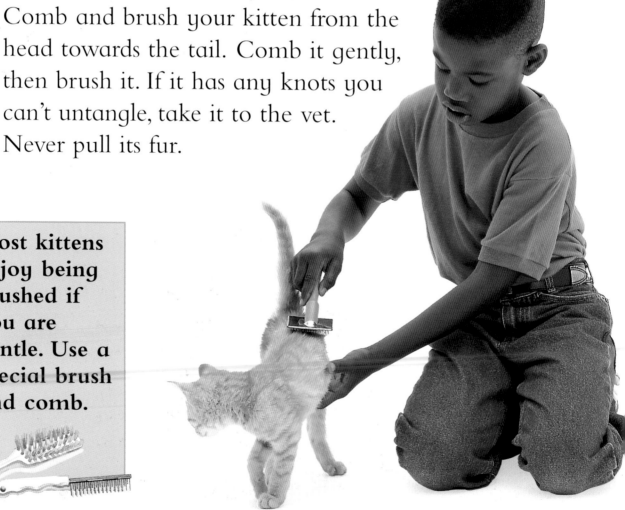

When long-haired kittens lick themselves they swallow loose hairs. The hairs can form a furball in a kitten's stomach and make it ill. If this happens, take your kitten to the vet.

If you groom your pet carefully, it should not get furballs.

If your kitten keeps scratching, it may have fleas. Ask your vet for help.

Kittens enjoy exploring and getting into mischief.

Kittens will explore their home from top to bottom. They climb on furniture and crawl under tables. Give your pet a box to explore.

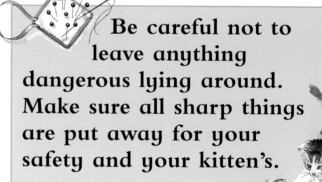

Be careful not to leave anything dangerous lying around. Make sure all sharp things are put away for your safety and your kitten's.

If your kitten scratches the furniture say 'no' in a firm voice. Buy it a scratching post from a pet shop. Never shout at or hit your kitten.

Make sure your kitten
doesn't eat indoor
flowers or plants
as these may be
poisonous.

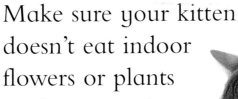

Before your kitten
explores outside, it will
need a collar with your
address or telephone
number on it. Make
sure the collar is an elastic
one and is not too tight.
Don't allow your kitten out
until it has
had all its
injections.

Your kitten will need to visit the vet.

A kitten should be taken to the vet for a check-up when it is about four weeks old. At 12 weeks it will need injections to stop it catching any diseases. It will need another injection every year.

All kittens should be neutered when they are about five months old. This is to prevent unwanted kittens.

If your kitten stops eating, keeps sneezing, has runny eyes or dry fur, it might be ill. Put it in a special carrier and take it to the vet straight away.

Cardboard carriers can be used for kittens and small cats. Bigger cats need stronger carriers.

How is your kitten feeling?

Your kitten will soon know your voice and smell. It may rub against you to say hello. If it holds its tail up in the air it is pleased to see you.

If your kitten is angry or frightened, it will make itself look bigger by arching its back and fluffing up its fur. Do not touch your kitten if it does this.

When your kitten licks your hand it is being friendly. If it kneads your lap or purrs it is happy.

When your kitten is hungry it will miaow. Some kittens raise a paw to beg. Older kittens may beg by standing on their back legs.

If your kitten feels safe, it may lie on its back. Don't tickle its tummy. Most kittens don't like having their tummy touched.

27

Your kitten will soon grow up.

When your kitten is about a year old you will see how grown up it looks. It will still enjoy playing, but be careful – it will have sharp teeth and claws.

As your cat grows older it will be less playful, and will sleep more. But it will still like being stroked and talked to.

Cats can live for 20 years or more, but like people they grow old and die. If your pet is very ill or badly injured it may also die.

You may feel sad when your pet dies, but you will be able to look back and remember all the happy times you had together.

Words to remember

fleas Tiny biting insects that live in a cat's fur.

groom To brush and comb a cat.

knead What a cat does when it pushes its claws in and out against something.

litter tray A cat's toilet.

mew The crying noise a very young kitten makes.

miaow The crying noise a cat makes.

paws Cats' feet.

pounce To jump on something suddenly.

purr The noise a cat makes in its throat.

suckling When a kitten drinks its mother's milk it is suckling.

vet An animal doctor.

whiskers The long hairs on a cat's face.

A newborn kitten cannot see or hear.

At three weeks a kitten is learning to walk.

At four weeks a kitten grows its first teeth.

At eight weeks a kitten is old enough to leave its mother.

Index

claws 28

feelings 26, 27, 29
fleas 21, 30
food 17

grooming 6, 20, 21

health 15, 21, 23

learning to walk 12–13
litter tray 16
long-haired cats 6, 21

plants 23
playing 14, 15
purring 11, 27

sleeping 17
suckling 11

tabby 7
teeth 28
tortoiseshell 7

vet 21, 24, 25

Notes for parents

A cat will give you and your family a great deal of pleasure, but it is a big responsibility. If you decide to buy a kitten for your child, you will need to ensure that the animal is healthy, happy and safe. You will have to train and feed your pet, and care for it if it is ill. You will also have to supervise your child with the animal until he or she is at least five years old. It will be your responsibility to make sure your child does not harm the kitten and learns to handle it correctly.

Here are some other points to think about before you decide to own a cat:

* Is your home suitable for a cat? Do you have a garden or will you have to keep a litter tray in the house all the time? Are you near a main road? If you have a balcony, do not let your cat out on to it.

* Do you have other pets? Will the kitten get on with them?

* Who will look after your cat when you go on holiday? Can you afford a cattery?

* Kittens and cats need annual injections. Can you afford them?

* If there is no one at home all day, it is better to have two cats together.

* All cats should be neutered. Make sure you can afford the vet's fees.

* Cats often bring dead or live animals, such as birds and mice, into the house.

* Cats can live for 20 years or more, and may need expensive treatment as they grow older. You can take out insurance.

* Cats can be microchipped to identify their owners. This may be safer and more reliable than wearing a collar.

This book is intended as an introduction only for young readers. If you have any queries about how to look after your kitten, you can contact the PDSA (People's Dispensary for Sick Animals) at Whitechapel Way, Priorslee, Telford, Shropshire TF2 9PQ. Tel: 01952 290999.